the Ruggermals

CHILDREN'S GUIDE

to: Rugby

A Children's Guide to Rugby

Dan'l Bair

Ruggermals

Dan'l Bair

Rugby is one amazing game! It may look confusing with so much going on and 30 folks running about at once, but it's not as hard to learn as it seems. It takes many different skills, and no matter what size or shape you may be, there is a position that is just right for every boy or girl. Everyone is allowed to run, pass, kick, tackle, ruck and maul.

During a match, rugby players wear shorts, long socks, and shoes with cleats/sprigs on the bottom often referred to as cleats or boots. But the most famous piece of a rugby uniform is the rugby jersey. The rugby jersey has changed over the years to include many different styles and colors. Some jerseys are even made of special material to keep players cool in the heat and warm in the cold. Usually a rugby jersey is made of strong cotton with different patterns of stripes for each team, and a collar with rubber buttons that won't scrape your skin or break into pieces.

Rugby is played on a field shaped like a rectangle with goalposts on each end, that look like the letter "H". Players try to score by placing the ball on the ground behind the opposing teams endline which is known as a try (5points) or kicking it through the goals (above the crossbar) at the ends of the field (2 points right after a try is scored, and 3 points from a dropgoal/ dropkick or penalty kick). You can kick or carry the ball any direction you like, but all passes must go backwards or sideways. Tackling by wrapping someone up with your arms until they fall to the ground is a big part of rugby, and the rough and tumble nature of the game can make it even more fun.

You can get as Muddy, Sweaty, Bumpy, and "Scrape-E" as you like and your parents won't even be upset with you. It's better than being a Sofapotamus any day!

Equipment

One of the nice things about rugby is that you don't need any silly equipment to participate, although a mouthpiece/gumshield is important.

Here are a few funny sounding rugby terms, which you may not have heard before.

SCRUM

With a forward pass
Or forward fumble

"Form the scrum"
The ref will grumble.

When the scrumhalf rolls it in
Foot it back so you can win

With all the forwards bound up tight
They drive as one with all their might

A scrum happens when someone accidentally drops the ball forward (Knock-on) or passes the ball forward. It looks like a strange interlocking puzzle of bodies. A scrumhalf rolls the ball in between forwards from each team who push each against each other to gain control of the ball using only their feet.

RUCK

The runner's tackled
But not out of luck
To keep the ball
They form the ruck!

A ruck happens when someone gets tackled and players try to push their opponents away from the pile to gain control of the ball.

MAUL

They're on their feet,
It's quite a brawl
Pushing and shoving
They drive the Maul....

A Maul happens when a tackler can't bring their opponent to the ground and nearby players begin pushing on the players involved in the tackle while they are still standing up.

LINEOUT

With a mighty kick the ball's gone out
Form your lines the hookers shout

The ball's thrown in straight and fair
While forwards jump into the air

With a skillful catch the job is done
The ball's secure
The lineout's won!

A lineout happens when the ball goes outside
the boundaries of the field and both teams form
lines and jump for the ball when it is thrown back
into play.

PENALTY KICK

The ref's caught on
  To a dirty trick
  And so awards
  A penalty kick.

A penalty kick is given to a team after an opponent has broken the rules. The team taking the kick can try to kick it at the goal for three points, kick it to themselves, or punt it off the field and then get to throw it back into the lineout where the ball went out of bounds.

POSITIONS

There are 15 players on a rugby team and each position has its own number and a special job to do. There are 8 big strong players who make up the "forwards", 6 often smaller and faster players known as "backs", and one player who forms a link between the two groups known as a halfback or scrumhalf.

THE FORWARDS

The pack form lineouts and the scrum
You want forwards
Well here they come....
They push and shove
They're big and strong
Watch the scrumhalf tag along

#1 & 3:

The Props form the front row of the scrum and "prop up" the hooker. In a Lineout you will find them lifting players who jump for the ball. They are usually the largest and stoutest players on a rugby team, so they provide a great deal of muscle when gaining possession of the ball.

#2:

The Hooker's job is to hook the ball back in the scrum, and throw the ball into the lineout. They are expected to lead by example and use their mobility and muscle all around the field. The hooker is usually the smallest Forward player.

Jean Boelter

1941-2010

lent of Amputeddy, Inc. until her battle with cancer
. in 2010, Jean was a counselor and advocate for
ees of all ages for many years. Her left leg was
d at the age of five. She dedicates these stories to
aany courageous people she met in her work.

Today was the day Todd the Amputeddy was going school. After his accident he had spent a lot of time hospital and at home. Now he was finally ready. He nervous as he waited for the bus.

door opened, he swallowed hard, gathered his
and stepped on.

ay at school, Todd was a little embarrassed. He
ryone was staring at his leg and the way he

But he was mostly glad to see his friends, and they to see him too.

They were all very curious about his new le

Todd was kind of afraid, but he nodded his h
anyway.

ot to the classroom, his teacher said, "We're very
 back and looking so well, Todd! Later during
 you can tell us all about your new leg and how it
?"

As share time grew nearer, Todd grew more and m
nervous. His paws started to sweat and he felt like
want to stand up in front of the class with his weird
leg.

Todd felt like going home.

But when the time came for him to share, and he fe
he remembered that he had already had to do mucl
things. He stood right up and pulled his leg right off
class all gasped in wonder. He told them about how
just for him and that it has lots of different names lil
leg, prosthesis, and dolly leg.

Then he put his helper leg back on and walked arou
room. Everyone clapped and cheered for him. He fe
special and he was so glad that he had shared.

By lunch Todd felt like a king! Everyone wanted to k
about his accident, what it was like in the hospital, a
it was like without his left foot. He got so much atter
he completely forgot about feeling so nervous befor

In line waiting for drinks at the water fountain, his fr
Suzie asked him, "Where did your leg go? Is it in you
at home?"

"No," he replied, "they took it away at the hospital. I
lot, but it's not coming back to hurt me ever again."

His first day back to school was one of the best days he could remember.

; got used to his new leg, and he didn't always feel
ıg every day, but he realized that things weren't
ifferent before his accident. He knew now that he
regular bear just like everyone else.

Jean Boelter, Kate Policani

The End

Dear Reader,

y, Inc. was donated by Jean Boelter to Harborview
enter's Limb Viability department upon her death.
e books to me, Kate Policani, as co-author.

ning all proceeds from the purchase of this book
pport Amputeddy, inc. and the limb loss support
arborview.

ore about other Amputeddy books and any news
the bears, please visit
policani.com/amputeddy-books/ .

se books fulfill their purpose to comfort and
 you or your loved one struggling with limb loss.
d have wanted to hear your story and share hers
hese stories were her story too.

vishes,
ani

Made in the USA
Lexington, KY
27 September 2012

nputeddy Goes Back to School

By Jean Boelter and Kate Policani

Illustrated by Marta Creswell

#4 & 5:

The Locks are sometimes called the "engine room" because they are expected to provide the biggest push in the scrum. Locks are also the main jumpers in the lineout. Being the tallest and usually biggest players in the Forwards, the locks are expected to do a mighty job and add some power to everything they do.

#6 & 7:

The Flankers are expected to do a lot of tearing about against the other forwards and backs weather they have the ball in hand or not. They only hold onto the sides of the scrum with 1 arm. The blind-side flanker (#6) tries to protect areas on the sides of the field, while the open-side (#7) flanker also helps protect against attacks from the other teams backs. You will also see flankers doing a variety of jobs in the lineout.

#8:

The Number 8 is another type of "Loose Forward" who can jump in lineouts, shove the scrum and do a great deal of carrying the ball forward against large players. The number 8 helps protect the Scrumhalf and is generally the largest loose forward.

LOOSE FORWARDS

6 BLIND SIDE FLANKER

7 FLANKER

OPEN SIDE

#8

23

#9:

The Scrumhalf is often the smallest player on the entire team, but they are expected to make some of the most important decisions and lead the forwards like a General leads an army. It is important to have an excellent pass and the courage to dive into a pile of the largest players to get the ball moving. It is one of the most exhausting and complicated positions in the game.

THE SCRUMHALF #9
Dig that BALL OUT!
PASS ON TARGET
#10
Get it Moving!
MARSHALL those TROOPS!

THE BACKS

The ball's secure but the job's not done
Send it wide, give the backs a run....!

#10:

The Flyhalf is the first in the line of backs who calls plays, leads the attack and makes important decisions about how to use the ball. They are usually among the best kickers in the game and must be a well-rounded and clever player no matter how big or small they are.

THE FLYHALF #10
LeAD that Attack!
Kick for Position
HAVE A Shot at GOAL!
10
10
10

#12 & 13:

The Centers are the biggest and most powerful backs, who try to run through gaps in the opposing defense and move the ball around in a way that confuses the other team. The Outside Center is usually a little faster, while the Inside Center should be the shiftier of the two. Both must be fearless and willing to crash into anything when necessary.

THE CENTERS
INSIDE #12 CENTER
OUTSIDE "13" CENTER
DEFEND that LINE
CRUNCH
WORK Together
FIND A GAP

#11 & 14:

The Wingers are the speed demons of the team who attack and defend down the sides of the field. They are the fastest players on the team and can sometimes be small like the Scrumhalf, Flyhalf and Fullback. The wingers need to work especially well with the Fullback and sometimes even act as scrumhalf.

#15:

The Fullback is another speedy player with extra quickness, an excellent kick and the courage to catch high kicks from the opposing team. As the last player in the back of the field, they must be excellent tacklers despite the fact that they are sometimes one of the smallest players on the field.

All in all, the key to winning a Rugby match is by playing together as a team no matter what your position is. Some players can play many different positions whereas others are only able play just one. It's best to try different things and find what's right for you. As you grow and change sometimes you will find that your favorite position will change too.

Either way,
if you get the chance,
give it a "Try"!

Last but not least, Rugby has a long tradition of honor and good sportsmanship, which we must never forget. This means that we do not use foul language, argue with the referee, taunt one another, or make a spectacle of ourselves when we play. In a real game of Rugby, hard work and fair play win the day. After a match all players shake hands, thank one another for their efforts and enjoy spending time with teammates, opponents and fans alike. Sportsmanship is very important and helps make Rugby the best game on earth!

The Final Whistle

(The End)

Since Rugby is a game played all around the world, different languages have different names for each position. Here are a few you can practice on your own.

Prop: Afrikaans-Stut, French-Pilier, Italian-Pilone, Spanish-Pilar, Irish-Taca, Welsh-Prop

Hooker: Afrikaans-Hakker, French-Talonneur, Italian-Tallonatore, Spanish-Talonador, Irish-Caiteoir, Welsh-Bachwr

Flanker: Afrikaans-Flank, French-Troisièmes Lignes, Italian-Terza Linea Fuori, Spanish-Tercera Línea, Irish-Tríú Líne, Welsh-Blaenasgellwr

Lock: Afrikaans-Slot, French-Deuxièmes Lignes, Italian-Seconda Linea, Spanish-Segunda Línea, Irish-Glas, Welsh-Clo

#8: Afrikaans-Agtsteman, French-Troisième Ligne Centre, Italian-Terza Linea Media, Spanish-Octavo, Irish-Uimhir a hocht, Welsh-Wythwr

Scrumhalf: Afrikaans-Skrumskakel, French-Demi de mêlée, Italian- Mediano di Mischia, Spanish-Medio Scrum, Irish-Leath chlibirt, Welsh-Mewnwr

Flyhalf: Afrikaans-Losskakel, French-Demi d'ouverture, Italian-Apertura, Spanish-Apertura, Irish-Eitilteoir, Welsh-Maswr

Center: Afrikaans-Senter, French-Centre, Italian-Centro, Spanish-Centro, Irish-Lár na páirce, Welsh-Canolwr

Wing: Afrikaans-Vleuel, French-Ailier, Italian-Ala, Spanish-Ala, Irish- Eiteoir, Welsh-Asgellwr

Fullback: Afrikaans-Heelagter, French-Arrière, Italian-Estremo, Spanish- Extremo o Zaguero, Irish-Lán chosantóir, Welsh-Cefnwr

Made in the USA
Lexington, KY
27 September 2012